*Illustrations by Regina Mills*

# Writings
## Of A
# Wild Woman

## Kelsea Cole

Copyright © Kelsea Cole 2020

All rights reserved.

# To Me:

I love you
More than
Anyone else.

# Table of Contents

○ The Darkness ............................................................. 1

○ The Dawn .................................................................. 25

○ The Light ................................................................... 57

# THE DARKNESS

# It's MY Story

This is *my* story.
I have the right to tell it *however I wish*.
If you have a problem with that,
Perhaps you should have behaved better in your role.

# 23

23 was
By far
The worst age
Of my life.

Not because
"Nobody liked me"
As the Blink-182
Song goes.

More so,
Because of
How deeply I
Did not like myself.

# Pitch Black

All-consuming
Never-ending
Potluck of misery.

Why can't this
Be the end
Of me?

# Lost Connection

I feel lost
Alone in the world
Like no one could understand
The thing that is my mind.

Sitting silently—
A room full of people
Playing on their phones.
No words being spoken.

What is life?
Why am I here?
Questions with no answers.
*Why do I keep asking?*

I can't be content,
No matter my surroundings.
I am an alien
Full of dissociation.

# Lemons

Everybody always says
*"When life gives you lemons,
Make lemonade."*

Nobody ever tells you
That after a while,
You'll get tired
Of the taste of lemonade.

# Poetic Thoughts

It has been quite a
while
since I painted poetic
words
on paper that
I was proud of.

I'll get out the pen
and notebook,
and sit there staring at blank
pages for what feels like
an eternity.

Yet, it is
probably only 60
seconds of misery...

I remember being young,
feeling free—
watching my hand move
across a hundred pages
a day sometimes—
with endless inspiration.

## Poetic Thoughts

Words would flow from my
mind to my hand without
thought or resistance.

It just was.
It was easy,
and it felt fantastic.

How do I get it
back?
Did I lose the spark, or is the
flame just burning low
in the background,
waiting for fuel?

# Parental Units

You taught me,
Slowly, but surely,
To kill all my dreams.

It's okay.
You meant to
Keep me safe.

You didn't want your
Day-dreamer daughter
To grow up as a
Starving Artist.

It took me 25
Years to realize
That the voices telling
Me not to TRY,
Sounded exactly
Like my mom & dad.

You taught me,
Slowly, but surely,
To kill all my dreams.

## Parental Units

Maybe it's because,
During the process
Of raising me,
You killed all your own
Life fantasies.

# Creative Expression

My dad reads books,
My mom watches TV.

Maybe if I can
Put my life in a book,
Or make it into a movie,
They will finally
Start to understand me.

# Gone

You were one
Of the best friends
I ever had—
Until all of a sudden,
You weren't.

# Warning

*Sweet girl,
you better watch out for those boys
with the sad eyes
and the long eyelashes.*

# Consent

*"No"*
**NEVER** means
*"Convince me."*

    —*That was rape.*

# Crazy

He used to call her
Crazy all the time.
Now I wonder
If he says it about me...

*-Manipulation will drive anyone insane.*

# Ghost

One day,
You were fully invested.
The next day,
I was ghosted.

*—You never gave me
the closure I deserved.*

# **Duped**

> But wait...
> *You complimented my soul!*
> And then,
> **You crushed it.**

# Self-Harm

Perhaps the worst way
I ever hurt myself
Was not the
Slicing of my skin.

Instead,
It was loving you
When I should
Have loved myself.

# Hoarder

You keep every little thing;
Nothing can ever leave you.

I look at everything
You've stashed over the years,
And wonder:
"What do you emotionally
Associate with this object
That makes it so impossible
To let go of?"

You don't know how to be free.

# J.W.

I'll never understand
Why you chose
To hold my heart,
Only long enough
To break it.
   —*Putting myself back together was the best revenge.*

# Yin & Yang

I have some angels at my shoulder—
Yet, I have lots of demons around the corner.
Balance, may it please be bestowed upon me.

# Universe

I woke up today,
    *Pissed at the world.*

        For I feel I have given
            This world *so much of myself,*
    & it keeps taking away from me.

    It will all even out
Somehow, someday.

# Losing Friends

I am hurt,
I am heartbroken
By the people of my past.
In my search for myself,
I found some fake friends
With sugar-coated words
Who made me feel higher than
The sky when we were together.

Drunken nights cloud my mind
Like they once clouded my judgement.
So many mistakes made; too much
Trust given to troublemakers and
Heartbreakers.

So much regret for the times
I let myself slip away for the sake
Of letting someone else in.

Oh, how I wish I could
Half-ass emotions,
Half-heartedly love.
How I wish I had loved myself

## Losing Friends

Before giving myself
Away to too many undeserving
Friends and "lovers."

How I wish I didn't choose
To seek out the good
In the worst of people.

How I wish I had been stronger
When friendships and relationships
Crumbled as quickly as they started.

How I wish I had protected
My childishly trusting heart
From becoming a punching bag
For all those who were angry
Enough with life to take a swing.

I was so undeserving
Of all the shadows cast upon me,
Clouding up my soul
And eating me up from the core.
How I wish I'd listened less
And observed a lot more.
Maybe then my mind and heart
Wouldn't be at such a terrible war.

# THE DAWN

# Less Traveled

Sitting here alone,
Wondering how I got here.

How did I lose
All my best friends
So quickly?

How did I let go
So easily?
Why did I choose to be
The best me?

Why do I keep
Choosing the path
Less traveled?

Why do I feel
Like I have to choose
Between my dreams
And the people I love?

Why do I get so scared
When I think about

## Less Traveled

Moving on from
What I know?

Why do my fears
Keep holding me
In one place?

The more I let go of,
The more I have to lose.
The more I let others go,
The more I find myself.

I know that
The right people,
The right opportunities,
The right thoughts
Will come with time.
When you're on the right path,
Nothing can ever "go wrong."

I will carry this truth
In my heart
And know that
Nothing will stop me
From living my dreams.

# Psychology

Learning more about
The effects of trauma
On the brain
Is both very empowering
And very depressing.

The effects of my childhood
Caused a chain reaction
Of patterns & decisions
That were normal
For my situation.

*Why doesn't this*
*Make me feel better?*

At the same time,
I know more now.
I am getting better.

# Forgiveness

I thought the
Hardest thing
I'd ever do
Was finally
Learning to
Forgive you.

Turns out, the
Hardest thing
Was
Forgiving
Myself for
Loving you.

# How I Heal

This is how I find my freedom,
this is how I move on.
This is how my soul releases the tension,
how I get all the bad feelings to be gone.

This is how I start fresh,
this is how I let go.
This is how I heal the parts of me
that not many people get to know.

So if my writing bothers you,
if it strikes a chord,
know that I have no remorse
for the healing that has come from this keyboard.

# 11/11/18

Someone I haven't connected
with for many moons
sent me a message today,
saying "I've missed you."

*Ah, yes.*
I've missed me too.

# Seasons

I wish I had some
Words to rhyme.
I wish I had good news
This time.

I wish I had fun, fabulous,
Fantastic things to say,
But I do not today.

I wanted to share
How great I'm doing,
How happy I am,
How amazing my life is.
But I simply have
Nothing of that sort to say.

My car broke down,
My debit card information got stolen,
And my money was taken.
A tree fell on the powerline
Outside my house,
And nearly caught it on fire,
Starting with my room.

## Seasons

The power is out,
The backup generator
Wouldn't work,
The heat was too much
For me to sleep last night.
My eyes have never hurt
From crying before this.

So, at least
Now I know that's possible.
That's a thing that can happen.

I have nothing much to say,
Except that when it
Rains,
It pours for hours.
And days.
And months.

Sometimes,
All we can do is
Remind ourselves that
Although it can't be sunshine
All the time,
It can't rain forever, either.

It's one thing
After the next,

## Seasons

After the next
After the next...

But still, I stand.
I remind myself that
*I am alive.*
*I am healthy.*
*I am safe.*
*I have food to eat.*
*I have people who love me.*
*Everything is okay.*

And on days like this,
Where I have nothing
Except those words
To remind myself that
My life is worth living,
I cry to my therapist
And she tells me that
It's only one season
In my lifetime.

Plus, this is Michigan,
So the season
Is about to change.

I will be okay.

# Have Faith

I have faith
That God will
Work everything
Out perfectly
All according to
The plan that is
Best for all
Involved.

Maybe it didn't
Work out the way
I wanted it to,
But God is smiling,
Knowing it is all
Working out
The way it is
Supposed to.

# Life

Patterns repeating...
What is the meaning?

*Have you learned this time?*

Repeat the unconscious—
Or will you shine?

# Environment

Maybe I'm not where I want to be.
    But I'll get there,
        *Eventually.*

# Watercolors

I'll never forget
the Light reflecting
on your face
as we drove
through the
majestic mountains
at dawn.

# Standards

If you think
The expectations
I set on you
Are too high,
Imagine the ones
I have for myself...

# Tiger Stripes

Stretch marks...
The beauty taboo.
Who taught us that
Proof of growing
Is ugly?

# Blurry Lines

My bad habits
Pull me back
Towards
The Darkness.

I know
Better now.
I don't have to
Fall for this.

# Fake Love

Shortly before
It all ended,
My ex snuck
A fake rose
Into my car,
With a note
That said:
*"I'll love you
Until it dies."*

Little did he
Understand,
That rose
Never
Had a life.

# The Other Woman

I'm sorry about
The battle over a boy
Who obviously never
Loved anything but
Drugs and sex.
   —*We are better than this.*

# Growth

You may never change,
and it's my job
to accept that.

# Lesson Learned

I can talk to you,
but I will never
trust you again.

# **Boundaries**

Until you're
finally ready to
    HEAR ME,
then I don't
want you anywhere
    NEAR ME.

# Disappeared

Like the wind,
I was there,
and then I was gone.
   *-These are my boundaries.*

# Love Bonds

Love may find you
In many forms
That you do not want
In order to show you
That which you do.

# Best Friend

I've always felt invisible,
In crowds or even
In tiny rooms of few people.
And yet,
I always wanted to stand out.

I wore crazy clothes
And asked a lot of questions,
More than other kids.
I carried around notebooks
And I wrote every thought
Inside the pages.
Seldom did I share them.

I probably didn't
Make it easy
For other kids
To want to like me.

I did have some good friends.
Maybe even some "best friends,"
But even my best friends
Had a better friend than me.

## Best Friend

I never had that
One person who:
Always got me,
Always stood by me,
Always checked in,
Always made time.

Will I ever
Get the type of best friend
That I try to be?
Someone understanding,
Always caring,
Calling just because
They thought of me?

I've spent years trying...
Checking in,
Making plans,
Showing up for people
Who probably wouldn't notice
If I stopped my efforts altogether.
Or at least, they wouldn't care.

So now, I spend my days alone,
And all my nights at work.
I try not to let myself
Think about how lonely
My life has become outside

## Best Friend

Of spending time with family
And my significant other.

It's okay to be alone.
It's okay to be a loner.
It's okay to only have your family,

Or no one at all.
Because at the end of the day,
**I have myself**
And I will be my own
Best friend.

# Healing

*"How are you feeling about it?"*

Better.
Less sad.
Still slightly sad,
But not in that
Earth-shattering kind of way.

# Expansion

Suddenly,
**my idea of me**
is no longer
so small.

# Crossing Over

*"This is where*
*The dysfunction ends,"*
I said,
Drawing an
Imaginary line
In the
Imaginary sand
Of my life.

And then,
**I stepped over it.**

# **AFFIRM**

Everything is happening as it is supposed to.
I am making my dreams come true.
I have not failed, only fumbled slightly.
It is all going to work out in time.
I can let go of the problems and expectations
And know there will be a grand outcome.

# Contrast

Without the
raging depths
of the Darkness,
I would have
never seen
the Light.

# THE LIGHT

# Can You Feel It?

I can feel it again, finally.
I thought I had lost it forever.
I fought with my mind for a year
To get it back.
But here it is...
I found it!
My inspiration, my will to
Move forward.

It's back. And it's stronger than
It ever has been.
It pushes me to wake up early,
To eat a good breakfast,
To get some work done,
To exercise,
To pray, meditate,
And explore.

## Can You Feel It?

Can you feel it too?

It's been trying to pull you in
So much lately.
It's been begging you
To create
To do better
To try harder
To make wiser choices.

*Can you feel it?*

# Shift

Suddenly, everything
*Feels different.*
I don't know why
It happened,
Or what exactly
"It" is…

But this shift
Of positivity is
Lighting up my life.
I am stepping into who
I'm meant to be.

# Growing

I dug myself
down into the ground,
deep enough
to bury me.

I thought
I wanted my
life to be over
permanently.

But somewhere
in that hole beneath
the Earth, I began
to spread my roots.

Next thing
I knew, I was
shooting up
towards the Light.

I guess sometimes
you truly need
to be buried
in order to **GROW.**

# **Bloom**

Like the roses,
I needed the rainstorms
In order
To grow.

Budding,
Blossoming,
And now,
I am blooming.

I will never
Regret my growth.

# Unanswered Questions

As I learn to shine
My Light brighter,
And all these toxic people
Fade away,
I wonder what was
So appealing
About me when I was
Living in Darkness
Anyway.

# Inner Critic

I am safe to pursue
My wildest dreams now.
I no longer have
To listen to you.

# Timing

It's all coming
Together,
Piece by piece.

# Wars

I've started wars on this body.
This body that has kept me warm
And sheltered my soul.

I've struck its skin
With blades of hate,
I've fed it until it wanted to explode,
I've starved it until it wanted to eat itself,
I've pushed it until it screamed
Out for me to stop.

I have not been kind to this body.
I've nearly destroyed it in
My never-ending search for perfection,
Never understanding that maybe
It was crafted perfectly for me,
To hold in this shining soul
And carry me where I need to go.

I've wreaked absolute havoc
On this body.
When it wanted love,
I showed it hate.

## Wars

When it wanted loving warmth,
I surrounded it with cold people.
When it wanted nourishment,
I gave it garbage.
When it wanted peace
I gave it more war.

I've been too hard on this body.
I pulled at my skin
Around my stomach
A thousand times
While staring at my reflection.

I've picked at pimples,
I've jiggled my extra skin,
I've cut and modified parts of it
That were better off left alone.

Then I covered scars with tattoos
And hoped that would be enough
To show it how sorry I was.

I've never really loved this body.
Not exactly the way it is.
Not when I was thin,
Not when I was thick,
Not when I was in-between.

## Wars

I've strived for a perfect figure
Rather than a healthy one
And then cried out or acted out when
I didn't get what I wanted.

I've learned to be softer to this body—
Stop yelling at its image in the mirror,
Stop telling it that it's lesser,
Or that someone's better,
Or that it could be better.
I've accepted it for what it is.
I've become kinder over time,
Because it has always been kind to me.

I've learned to accept this body.
Because this body has carried
My heart through its breaking point.
Because it survived falls,
Breaks, hate, misuse and abuse
That I put it through.

I've learned to love this body.

Because it is mine.
Because it has worked hard,
Because it has fought off disease
Because it keeps surprising me.
Its will to survive,

## Wars

Despite the toxic
Brain it carried
All those years
Is amazing.

I have come to
Love my body.
I have formed a friendship with it.
I have stopped waging wars against it.
Because it has always been fighting for me,
And because it never deserved it
To begin with.

I'm sorry for the pain
I had to put it through,
But I am thankful
For where we stand today
With our peace treaty.

*No more wars*
*Of me against me.*

# Self-Love Poem

Loving yourself can be a lifelong battle.

I was doing so well
And had so much confidence—
Then, doubt crept in
and clouded my mind.

Yet, I kept fighting
For myself,
Stopped fighting so hard
Against myself.

Now, I wake up daily
And I affirm
 *"I love myself,*
 *I am happy.*
 *I am healthy.*
 *I have everything I need.*
 *I am worthy of all the*
 *Good coming my way.*
 *I make good decisions for myself.*
 *I choose nourishing things*
 *In my life."*

# Self-Love Poem

I wake up
And remind myself.
Because in this world
Where we are sold perfection
On magazines and on big screens,
It can be so hard not to compare,
Not to fall back into old,
Negative thought patterns,
To forget that you are
Perfect the way you were made.
> *Your body is perfect for you.*
> ***Affirm: My body is perfect for me.***

We must treat these bodies well,
And love them fully.
Wake up, affirm that you
Love yourself,
Nourish your body
With self-love and a healthy diet,
Some regular stretching,
And meditation.

> You are worth it.
> ***Affirm: I am worth it.***

# Acceptance

Our spirits are shaken,
Caught in the cages
Of human flesh.

Our souls are screaming out,
Begging for our attention.

Do you hear them?

They whisper to you while
You're sleeping, saying
*"Wake up, wake up, wake up!"*

They wish to take loving
Control of our bodies,
So our minds may find peace.

It can be scary at first,
To accept that there is a soul
Energy attached to your body.

But it's always been there.
It's always begging you
To make the best choices.
To nourish yourself;
Feed your mind, body, spirit
With the healthiest ingredients.

Are you listening to your soul?
Do you ever get quiet
Enough to hear its voice?

Close your eyes,
Hush your heart,
Relax your body,
***AND LISTEN.***

# Reminders

*"You've come such a long, long way."*

Ah, yes! I have.

*And I'll go even further...*

# Align

Stretching to the sky,
Bones cracking,
Sockets popping,
Exposing my aging body.

I feel myself
Centering,
Grounding,
Morphing into who
I'm meant to be.
—*I am living authentically.*

# Minimalism

I finally minimalized
Everything I own.
I've never felt so Light,
I've never felt so free.

I never realized how much
I was truly holding onto,
Stored in the closets
Of my home and mind.

I am now proud of the space
I take up in this universe.

# Peaking

The options are
> Infinite.

I can
> *Go anywhere*
> *Do anything*
> *Be anyone*
> I want to.

# **Ascended**

One day, I was
gently plucked
from my home
here on Earth,
and dropped
directly into
Heaven.

# Answers

Once I finally
Stopped searching,
All the answers
Came to me.

*—They were inside
me all along.*

# Found

I no longer
have to hide,
for I have
found myself.

# Thick Skin

As I look at
All the layers
You use to
Cover up
That screaming
Child inside you,
I wonder who
It was that
Made you think
Hiding your Light
Was the way to live.

# Generational Patterns

It ran in my family,
Until it ran into me.
I changed *everything*.

# Wild Woman

I will always be
A wild woman
Who loves plants
And their powers,
Sniffs essential oils,
Kisses little animals,
And thrives to
Connect with nature.

I will always be
A flower child,
A dirty hippie,
A tree-hugger,
Shining my unique
Light for all to see.

I will always be
A wild woman,
Writing about what
Makes me feel free.

# Creativity

You are the
Connection
Between
My experiences
And
My aspirations

*—You fill that gap*

# Confessions

Today,
I showered all
The shame away,
And opened up
About what
I've been through.

The inner child
Resting inside
My chest
Is rejoicing
That I finally
Spoke her truth.

# **Secrets**

Finally,
All my secrets
Have come out.
I am free
To just be me.

# Grandma

She held me
While I cried,
And whispered
*"I believe you."*

I thanked her
For listening.
She thanked me
For sharing.

# Gravity

The heaviness of this
"New reality"
Will not
Consume me.

Repeat:
*"I am free."*

# Hard Conversations

The conversations
That are
The hardest to have
Are always
The most
Necessary.

*-Speak up*
*for yourself*

# Fear

It's hard not to be afraid sometimes.
If I tried to list on paper
everything I was *afraid* of,
surely I could have written a novel
of **FEARS**.
I found that the more *Fearless*
I became in life,
the more reckless of decisions I made.

When I wasn't afraid of anything,
I started ruining
everything around me.

When I was afraid of everything,
I shut myself away,
fearing every move I made,
every word I would say.

Nowadays, I just accept the Fear.
I look it in the face
and say: *"You don't control me anymore."*
Fear is meant to keep us safe.
That is its purpose.

## Fear

But if we let it take over,
it will cripple all
chances of happiness.

Fear is like
an abandoned theme park,
slowly being taken over by weeds.
Persistent,
pressing against what once was
and what could be,
ruining the chances of true growth
for the park.

A friend once told me
When I was afraid to make a decision:
"FEAR is just
False
Evidence
Appearing
Real."

She was right...
My Fear was fake.
I had to get out of my own way.
Fear was something I made up
in my mind to
*"keep me safe,"* to keep me

# Fear

from feeling more heartbreak
or rejection.

Yet, slowly, I started
chopping away at the weeds
surrounding the theme park
that is my mind.
I turned the power back on,
started the rides back up,
tested the caramel apples,
and I let all the people back in.

My theme park was just fine,
and I finally let myself have a good time.

All I had to do, was chop away
at the weeds, spray a little weed-killer,
accept that there were some spots
where weeds would always grow,
and make sure they didn't take over
my theme park once again.

# Empathy

It is beautiful
To feel so deeply,
But I will
No longer accept
Other's emotions
As my own.

*—Boundaries require practice,
but they are worth it.*

# **Roses**

My new lover
wants to grow
a garden full
of roses
with me
to nourish
forever.

# Lover

Hold me like your favorite softcover,
Caress me like I'm made of paper,
Promise never to tear me apart.

# Poetry

You comfort me
with sweet strings of words
when no one else
is around.

# Wrinkled

One hand under water,
The other flipping
Pages of poetry.

When the book is finished,
I meet my
Hands together.

A smooth surface
Against a wrinkled one.
A stark reminder
Of what it would have
Been like if
I had stayed
Submerged
Forever.

# Soulmate

*"Never stop writing,"*
he said,
and I fell
deeper in love.

# Lend You Light

If you're living
in Darkness right now,
let me lend you
a little of
my Light
to spark yours
back to life.

# Awareness

Breathe.

Be here, now.

You'll never
Get this
Moment again.

# Therapy

The greatest tool
I've received
While on my
Healing journey is
Without a doubt:
Therapy.

I wish
Everyone
Had access
To this magical
Form of healing.

*-With it, we could build
a better world.*

# Release

It's okay to:
    *Let go*
*Let live*
    *Fall in love again*
*Enjoy yourself*
    *Love yourself*
*Take care of yourself*
    *Be yourself*

Please
Release all belief
That says otherwise.

# **Vision**

Have you ever wanted something
So badly
That you would stop
At nothing
To get it?

Have you ever worked at something
So hard
Because you could not
Imagine your life
Without it?

Have you ever stayed up all night
Worrying about something
So much
Because you were scared
It wasn't going to work out?

Have you ever wanted success
More than
You wanted to breathe?
Have you ever decided
*Now is the time*

## Vision

To be making memories
Instead of dreams?

I see it on the horizon:
Everything I've ever wanted.
Do I have the guts
To grab it by the horns
And pull it towards me?

I will make my dream
My reality.
*You'll see.*

# **Abundance**

I am actively
attracting abundance
into my life.
It was time to
let go
of the fear mindset
& welcome more
Light into my space instead.

I still feel the Fear,
every single day.
But I feel this Fear,
and I do the thing
anyway.

# The End Of Winter

Looking behind me is so gloomy...
What's in front of me is so bright.

# Yellow

The future
is burning
so brightly
that I cannot
look at it
for too long.

# **Goals**

One by one,
*Crossing things*
Off the list.

> *—I will have to make
> new lists soon*

# Niche

Figuring out,
Slowly but surely,
Where I'm meant to be.

# Heard

All I ever
Wanted was
For someone
To hear me.

I have been
Screaming,
But there's
No sound
Traveling.

No matter
How loud
I got,
I always felt
Unheard.

Until now,
Until you
Read all
My words.

# Writings Of A Wild Woman

You started as a dream...
Something calling to me.
You turned into a blog,
And then a book.
What will you end up as?

# **To You:**

I hope these
Pages have
Filled you
With hope
And desire
To pursue
Your best you.

I hope
You fall
In love
With every
Part of who
You are.

You deserve it.

# Acknowledgements

I have to start by thanking my amazing partner, and biggest supporter, Devin Klein. You have never doubted the brilliance of my mind and art. You always encourage me to do whatever it is that my heart desires. Without you, I may never have achieved my dream of being a published author. Thank you for respecting the time I set aside for writing, and for always making my dreams come true.

In addition, my cousin Cory was a huge supporter in the process of writing this book. She read every single line (probably more than once), helped me with poem placement—and so much more—for MONTHS before this book was even close to publishing. I appreciate your support and your set of eyes on this masterpiece of mine.

My editing team: Kelli! Thank you for being the extra set of eyes, and bringing your English degree to the editing process. You truly crafted this book into what it is. You've read my books since we were 14, and I appreciate you still being on board with the process at 25. You'll always get a copy of my writings, as long as you want them! I also would like to give a shoutout to Eva, who did the final edit, and gave me such positive feedback, that I cried happy tears.

# Acknowledgements

Regina Mills: Thank you for your artistic support, your creativity, your kindness, and simply for being you! Your drawings bring the entire poetry collection together, and I'm so grateful we can work together as artists, and friends.

Channing...Thank you. You know for what, and I'll probably never stop thanking you. You're truly an Angel, a channel of God.

Teachers: Ms. Childs! My English teacher from middle school and my writing buddy! Thank you for encouraging my writing process over the years, and for reading all my angsty journals! Also, Ms. Roehrich, Ms. Smith, Mr. Goodwin, and Ms. Kolody—amazing teachers who supported my talents and creativity. You all made a difference for this old student!

Additionally, I would like to thank the other artists and creatives who helped make this come together. Emily, for your cover art, and Richa for your formatting abilities. You two put the final touches on this project!

To my family: Thanks for your ongoing support, no matter what crazy adventure I decide to take in this big, wide world. I will always be the wild woman you all raised me to be. I hope I make you proud.

# About The Author

Kelsea Cole began writing songs at the age of 5 and then never stopped writing. By the time she was 12, she was cranking out several new poems a week and creating her own novels. It's been a lifelong dream of hers to become a published writer. This book actualized that dream.

These days, Kelsea is a 25-year-old hippie and artist based in Northern Michigan. She is currently studying for a bachelor degree in Psychology, with a minor in Writing. Her passions are to use her creativity to help others in their own unique healing journeys, and sustainability.

# About The Author

Kelsea spends most of her days writing, cooking delicious plant-based meals, doing yoga, talking to her houseplants, blogging, and day-dreaming.

Check out the blog, PlantCenteredHealing.com.
Follow on Instagram, Facebook, and Pinterest @ plantcenteredhealing
Follow on Twitter and Medium @kelseawrites

www.ingramcontent.com/pod-product-compliance
Lightning Source LLC
Chambersburg PA
CBHW031450040426
42444CB00007B/1042